To: _____

From: _____

The Helen Steiner Rice Foundation

Whatever the celebration, whatever the day, whatever the event, whatever the occasion, Helen Steiner Rice possessed the ability to express the appropriate feeling for that particular moment in time. A happening became happier, a sentiment more sentimental, a memory more memorable because of her deep sensitivity and ability to put into understandable language the emotion being experienced.

Her positive attitude, her concern for others, and her love of God are identifiable threads woven into her life, her work . . . and even her death.

Prior to Mrs. Rice's passing, she established the Helen Steiner Rice Foundation, a nonprofit corporation that awards grants to worthy charitable programs assisting the elderly and the needy.

Royalties from the sale of this book will add to the financial capabilities of the Helen Steiner Rice Foundation. Because of limited resources, the foundation presently restricts grants to qualified charitable programs in Lorain, Ohio, where Helen Steiner Rice was born, and Greater Cincinnati, Ohio, where Mrs. Rice lived and worked most of her life.

Because of her foresight, caring, and deep convictions of sharing, Helen Steiner Rice continues to touch a countless number of lives through foundation grants and her inspirational poetry.

Thank you for your assistance in helping to keep Helen's dream alive and growing.

ANDREA E. CORNETT, ADMINISTRATOR

CELEBRATIONS
of the HEART

HELEN STEINER RICE

Fleming H. Revell
A Division of Baker Book House Co
Grand Rapids, Michigan 49516

© 1987 by the Helen Steiner Rice Foundation

Published by Fleming H. Revell
a division of Baker Book House Company
P.O. Box 6287, Grand Rapids, MI 49516-6287

New edition published 2001

Printed in the United States of America

Library of Congress Cataloging-in-Publication Data

Rice, Helen Steiner.
    Celebrations of the heart / Helen Steiner Rice.—2nd ed.
      p. cm.
    ISBN 0-8007-1777-5 (cloth)
      1. Christian poetry, American. I. Title.
    PS3568.I28 C4 2000
    811'.54—dc21   00-039020

Jacket photo and photos on pages 34 and 46 by Beth Ludwig-Khalfayan.

Jacket and interior designed by Robin K. Black.

For current information about all releases from Baker Book House, visit our web site:

http://www.bakerbooks.com

We all need words to live by,
   to inspire us and guide us,
Words to give us courage
   when the trials of life betide us.
And the words that never fail us
   are the words of God above,
Words of comfort and of courage
   filled with wisdom and with love.

SPRING

The Waking Earth

The waking earth in springtime
reminds us it is true
That nothing really ever dies
that is not born anew.
So trust God's all-wise wisdom
and doubt the Father never,
For in His heavenly kingdom,
there is nothing lost forever.

Beyond the Clouds

Most of the battles of life are won
By looking beyond the clouds to the sun,
And having the patience to wait for the day
When the sun comes out and the clouds float away!

All nature heeds the call of spring
As God awakens everything.

Spring Song

"The earth is the Lord's
   and the fullness thereof,"
It speaks of His greatness,
   it sings of His love.
And the wonder and glory
   of the first Easter morn,
Like the first Christmas night
   when the Savior was born,
Are blended together
   in symphonic splendor
And God with a voice
   that is gentle and tender
Speaks to all hearts
   attuned to His voice,
Bidding His listeners
   to gladly rejoice.
For He who was born
   to be crucified
Arose from the grave
   to be glorified.
And the birds in the trees
   and the flowers of spring
All join in proclaiming
   this heavenly King.

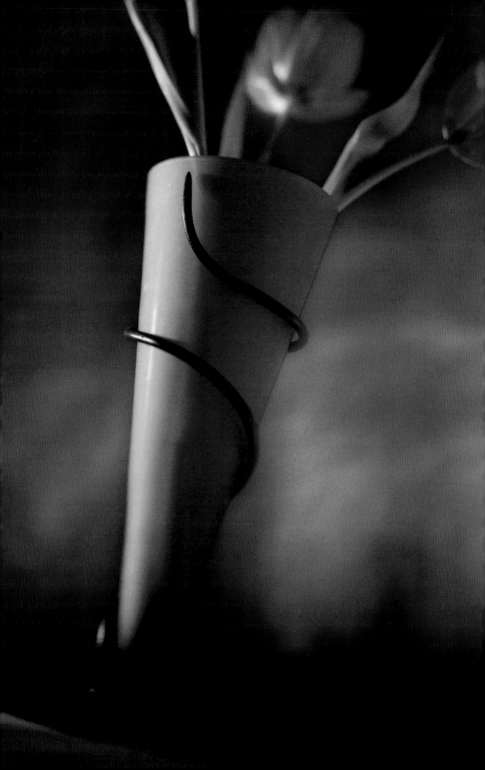

Spring Awakens
What Autumn Puts to Sleep

A garden of asters of varying hues,
Crimson pinks and violet blues,
Blossoming in the hazy fall,
Wrapped in autumn's lazy pall.
But early frost stole in one night,
And like a chilling, killing blight,
It touched each pretty aster's head
And now the garden's still and dead,
And all the lovely flowers that bloomed
Will soon be buried and entombed
In winter's icy shroud of snow—
But, oh, how wonderful to know
That after winter comes the spring
To breathe new life in everything.
And all the flowers that fell in death
Will be awakened by spring's breath,
For in God's plan both men and flowers
Can only reach "bright, shining hours"
By dying first to rise in glory
And prove again the Easter story.

The Glory of the Easter Story

In the glorious Easter story
    a troubled world can find
Blessed reassurance
    and enduring peace of mind.
For though we grow discouraged
    in this world we're living in,
There is comfort just in knowing
    God has triumphed over sin,
For our Savior's resurrection
    was God's way of telling men
That in Christ we are eternal
    and in Him we live again.
And to know life is unending
    and God's love is endless too
Makes our daily tasks and burdens
    so much easier to do,
For the blessed Easter story
    of Christ the living Lord
Makes our earthly sorrow nothing
    when compared with this reward.

Rejoice! It's Easter!

"Let not your heart be troubled,"
let not your soul be sad,
Easter is a time of joy
when all hearts should be glad—
Glad to know that Jesus Christ
made it possible for men
To have their sins forgiven
and, like Him, to live again.
So at this joyous season
may the wondrous Easter story
Renew our faith so we may be
partakers of His glory!

The Miracles of Easter

The sleeping earth awakens,
  the robins start to sing,
The flowers open wide their eyes
  to tell us it is spring.
The bleakness of the winter
  is melted by the sun,
The tree that looked so stark and dead
  becomes a living one.
These miracles of Easter,
  wrought with divine perfection,
Are the blessed reassurance
  of our Savior's resurrection.

A Special Prayer for Easter

God, make us aware
that the Savior died
And was nailed to a cross
and crucified
Not to redeem
just a chosen few
But to save all who ask
for forgiveness from You.

A Crown of Stars

Oh, spare me all trouble and save me from sorrow,
May each happy day bring a brighter tomorrow.
May I never know pain or taste bitter woe,
Sadness and suffering I care not to know.
But if I should meet Him sometime face to face,
Will I feel oddly strange and a bit out of place,
When I look at the marks where the nails went in
As He hung on the cross to save us from sin?
Will He think me unworthy to be one of His own
And too weak and untried to sit at His throne?
Will I forfeit my right to a crown set with stars
Because I can show Him no "battle scars"?
Will the one who suffered and wept with pain
Be the one He will welcome to share His domain?
Will the trials of life make a crown of stars
Unfit to be worn by one without scars?

Let Us Pray on This Holy Easter Day

Let our prayer continue
    through a joyous waking spring
In thanking God for everything
    a newborn spring can bring.
And in the resurrection
    that takes place in nature's sod
Let us understand more fully
    the risen Savior, Son of God.
And let us see the beauty
    and the glory and the grace
That surrounds us in the springtime
    as the smiling of God's face.
And through a happy springtime
    and a summer filled with love
May we walk into the autumn
    with our thoughts on God above.
The God who sends the winter
    and wraps the earth in death
Will always send the springtime
    with an awaking breath
To every flower and leaflet
    and to every shrub and tree
And that same God will also send
    new life to you and me.

The Easter Story

He was crucified and buried,
　　but today the whole world knows
The resurrection story
　　of how Jesus Christ arose.
Some may question it and doubt it,
　　but they can't explain or say
Why after countless centuries
　　we still follow Christ today.
And they miss the peace and comfort
　　that the Easter story brings,
The promise of eternal life
　　and the hope for better things.
For just to know the Savior died
　　to redeem and save all men,
And that because He gave His life,
　　we too shall live again,
Makes all this world's uncertainties,
　　its burdens, care, and strife
Seem meaningless when they're compared
　　to God's eternal life.
And Easter, as it comes each year
　　to awaken the sleeping earth,
Assures us all that Jesus Christ
　　has promised us rebirth.

The Promise of Easter

"Because He lives we too shall live"—

We need these seven words above
    to help us to endure
The changing world around us
    that is dark and insecure,
To help us view the present
    as a passing episode,
A troubled, brief encounter
    on life's short and troubled road.
For knowing life's eternal
    because our Savior died
And rose again at Easter
    after He was crucified
Makes this uncertain present
    in a world of sin and strife
Nothing but a stepping-stone
    to a new and better life!

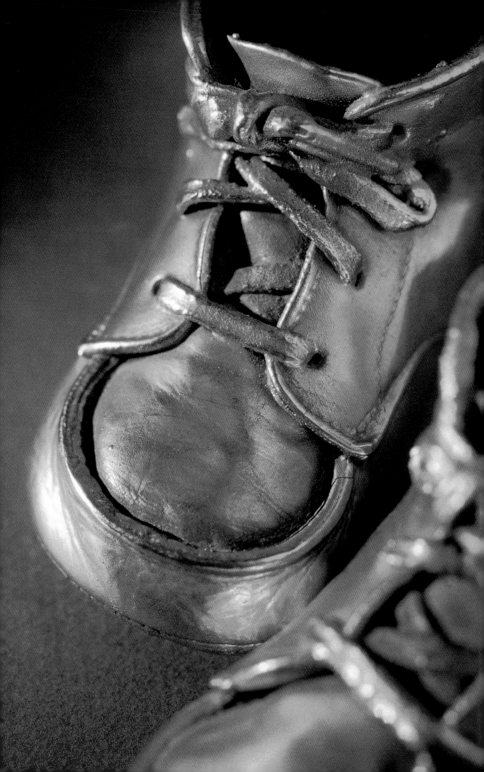

Mother Is a Word Called Love

Mother is a word called love,
And all the world is mindful of
The love that's given and shown to others
Is different from the love of mothers.
For mothers play the leading roles
In giving birth to little souls,
For though "small souls" are heaven-sent
And we realize they're only lent,
It takes a mother's loving hands
And her gentle heart that understands
To mold and shape this little life
And shelter it through storm and strife.
No other love than mother love
Could do the things required of
The one to whom God gives the keeping
Of His wee lambs, awake or sleeping.
So mothers are a "special race"
God sent to earth to take His place,
And mother is a lovely name
That even saints are proud to claim.

Mother's Day Is Remembrance Day

Mother's Day is remembrance day,
    and we pause on the path of the year,
To pay honor and worshipful tribute
    to the mother our heart holds dear.
For whether here or in heaven,
    her love is our haven and guide,
For always the memory of mother
    is a beacon light shining inside.
Time cannot destroy her memory
    and years can never erase
The tenderness and the beauty
    of the love in a mother's face.
And when we think of our mother,
    we draw nearer to God above,
For only God in His greatness
    could fashion a mother's love.

What Is a Mother?

It takes a mother's love
   to make a house a home,
A place to be remembered,
   no matter where we roam.
It takes a mother's patience
   to bring a child up right,
And her courage and her cheerfulness
   to make a dark day bright.
It takes a mother's thoughtfulness
   to mend the heart's deep hurts,
And her skill and her endurance
   to mend little socks and shirts.
It takes a mother's kindness
   to forgive us when we err,
To sympathize in trouble
   and bow her head in prayer.
It takes a mother's wisdom
   to recognize our needs
And to give us reassurance
   by her loving words and deeds.

A Mother's Love

A mother's love is something
  that no one can explain,
It is made of deep devotion
  and of sacrifice and pain.
It is endless and unselfish
  and enduring come what may,
For nothing can destroy it
  or take that love away.
It is patient and forgiving
  when all others are forsaking,
And it never fails or falters
  even though the heart is breaking.
It believes beyond believing
  when the world around condemns,
And it glows with all the beauty
  of the rarest, brightest gems.
It is far beyond defining,
  it defies all explanation,
And it still remains a secret
  like the mysteries of creation—
A many-splendored miracle
  we cannot understand
And another wondrous evidence
  of God's tender guiding hand.

Motherhood

The dearest gifts that heaven holds,
  the very finest too,
Were made into one pattern
  that was perfect, sweet, and true.
The angels smiled, well pleased, and said,
  "Compared to all the others,
This pattern is so wonderful
  let's use it just for mothers!"
And through the years a mother
  has been all that's sweet and good,
For there's a bit of God and love
  in all true motherhood.

A PRAYER FOR THOSE LOST IN BATTLE

Give eternal rest to them, O Lord,
  whose souls have taken flight
And lead them to a better world
  where there is peace and light.
Grant them eternal freedom
  from conflict, war, and care,
And fulfill for them Thy prophecy,
  "There shall be no night there."

SUMMER

The Comfort
and Sweetness of Peace

After the clouds, the sunshine,
  after the winter, the spring,
After the shower, the rainbow,
  for life is a changeable thing.
After the night, the morning,
  bidding all darkness cease,
After life's cares and sorrows,
  the comfort and sweetness of peace.

The Seasons of the Soul

When you feel cast down and despondently sad
And you long to be happy and carefree and glad,
Do you ask yourself, as I so often do,
Why must there be days that are cheerless and blue?
Why is the song silenced in the heart that was gay?
And then I ask God, "What makes life this way?"
And His explanation makes everything clear—
The soul has its seasons, the same as the year.
We, too, must pass through life's autumn of death
And have our hearts frozen by winter's cold breath.

But spring always comes with new life and birth
Followed by summer to warm the soft earth.
And, oh, what a comfort to know there are reasons,
That souls, like nature, must too have their seasons—
Bounteous seasons and barren ones too,
Times for rejoicing and times to be blue.
For with nothing but "sameness" how dull life would be,
For only life's challenge can set the soul free,
And it takes a mixture of both bitter and sweet
To season our lives and make them complete.

God's Gifts Are Bountiful

We ask for a cupful
   when the vast sea is ours,
We pick a small rosebud
   from a garden of flowers.
Whatever we ask for
   falls short of God's giving,
For His greatness exceeds
   every facet of living.

The Center of the Flame

In the center of the flame
   there is a hollow place,
And nothing can burn
   in this sheltered space.
For the fire builds a wall,
   scientific fact claims,
And ensures a safe area
   in the midst of the flames.
And in the hurricane's fury
   there's a center of peace
Where the winds of destruction
   suddenly cease.
And this same truth prevails
   in life's tribulations,
There's an island of calm
   in the soul's meditations—
A place that is quiet
   where we're shielded from harms
Secure in the haven
   of a kind Father's arms

Where the hot flames of anger
    have no power to sear
And the high winds of hatred
    and violence and fear
Lose all the wrath
    and their savage course
Is softly subdued
    as faith weakens force.
So when the fires of life
    burn deep in your heart
And the winds of destruction
    seem to tear you apart,
Seek that small haven
    and be guided by prayer
To that place of protection
    within God's loving care.

The Key to Serenity

When you know and believe
without question or doubt
That in all you do
God is there to help out,
You hold in your hand the golden key
to peace and joy and serenity.

I Come to Meet You

I come to meet you, God, and as I linger here,
I seem to feel Your presence, and You are very near.
A rustling leaf, a rolling slope,
Speak to my heart of endless hope.
The sun just rising in the sky,
The waking birdlings as they fly,
The grass all wet with morning dew
Are telling me I've just met You!
And gently thus the day is born
And night gives way to breaking morn,
And once again I've met You, God,
And worshiped on Your holy sod.
For who can see the dawn break through
Without a glimpse of heaven and You?
For who but God could make the day
And softly put the night away?

Let Daily Prayers Dissolve Your Cares

We all have cares and problems
    we cannot solve alone,
But if we go to God in prayer
    we are never on our own.
And if we try to stand alone,
    we are weak and we will fall,
But God is always greatest
    when we're helpless, lost, and small.
And no day is unmeetable
    if on rising our first thought
Is to thank God for the blessings
    that His loving care has brought.
For there can be no failures
    or hopeless, unsaved sinners
If we enlist the help of God
    who makes all losers winners.
So meet Him in the morning
    and go with Him through the day
And thank Him for His guidance
    each evening when you pray.

And if you follow faithfully
    this daily way to pray
You will never in your lifetime
    face another hopeless day,
For like a soaring eagle
    you too can rise above
The storms of life around you
    on the wings of prayer and love.

Remember These Words

We are gathered together
　　on this happy day
To stand before God
　　and to reverently say,
I take thee to be
　　my partner for life,
To love and to live with
　　as husband and wife;
To have and to hold
　　forever, Sweetheart,
Through sickness and health
　　until death do us part;
To love and to cherish
　　whatever betide,
And in better or worse
　　to stand by your side.
We do this not lightly
　　but solemnly, Lord,
Asking Thy blessing
　　as we live in accord
With Thy holy precepts,
　　which join us in love,
And assure us Thy guidance
　　and grace from above.

And grant us, dear Lord,
   that "I will" and "I do"
Are words that grow deeper
   and more meaningful too
Through long, happy years
   of caring and sharing,
Secure in the knowledge
   that we are preparing
A love that is endless
   and never can die
But finds its fulfillment
   with You in the sky.

Love One Another

Love works in ways
    that are wondrous and strange,
There is nothing in life
    that love cannot change—
Love is unselfish,
    understanding, and kind,
Love sees with the heart
    and not with the mind.
And there's no stronger bond
    between husband and wife
To ensure and secure
    a blessed married life
Than to daily seek guidance
    from the Father above
And to meet what life brings
    with faith, trust, and love.

With Faith

With faith in each other
and faith in the Lord
May your marriage be blessed
with love's priceless reward,
For love that endures
and makes life worth living
Is built on strong faith
and unselfish giving.
So have faith that the Lord
will guide you both through
The glorious new life
that is waiting for you.

The Bond of Love

It takes a special day like this
To just look back and reminisce
And think of all the things you've shared
Since that first day you knew you cared.
Of course things change for that is life
And love between a man and wife
Cannot remain romantic bliss
Forever flavored with a kiss,
But always there's that bond of love
There's just no explanation of,
And with the storms and trials it grows
Like flowers do beneath the snows.
Sometimes it's hidden from the sight
Just like the sun gets lost in night,
But always there's that bond of love
There's just no explanation of.
And every year that you're together,
Regardless of the kind of weather,
The bond of love grows that much stronger
Because you've shared it one year longer.

You've Come a Long Way

You've come a long way
    over smooth roads and rough,
But you've had each other
    and that was enough,
For even the darkest
    and stormiest weather
Brings a rainbow of love
    when you share it together.
And because you have shared
    your smiles and your tears
You've built up rich treasures
    in these many years,
For the memories of things
    you've both shared and faced
Are engraved in your hearts,
    and they can't be erased.
And life with its problems
    has been but the blending
Of a love that's divine
    and therefore unending,

For love that endures
    through a long earthly life
And keeps folks together
    as husband and wife
Does not come and go
    with the physical form
And cannot be lost
    in the sun or the storm,
For it has become
    an intangible part
Of the soul and the spirit
    as well as the heart,
And because it's eternal
    such love never dies
For it is the kind
    you take to the skies,
And the world would be better
    and more lovely by far
If all married couples
    were the kind that you are.

Fathers Are Wonderful People

Fathers are wonderful people,
  too little understood,
And we do not sing their praises
  as often as we should,
For Father struggles daily
  to live up to his image
As protector and provider
  and hero of the scrimmage,
And perhaps that is the reason
  we sometimes get the notion
That fathers are not subject
  to the thing we call emotion.
But if you look inside Dad's heart,
  where no one else can see,
You'll find he's sentimental
  and as soft as he can be.

Fathers are just wonderful
    in a million different ways,
And they merit loving compliments
    and accolades of praise,
For the only reason Dad aspires
    to fortune and success
Is to make the family proud of him
    and bring them happiness,
And like our heavenly Father,
    he's a guardian and a guide,
Someone we can count on
    to be always on our side.

AUTUMN

A Prayer of Thanks

Thank You, God, for the beauty
around me everywhere,
The gentle rain and glistening dew,
the sunshine and the air,
The joyous gift of feeling
the soul's soft, whispering voice
That speaks to me from deep within
and makes my heart rejoice.

Give Thanks Every Hour

We all have many things
to be deeply thankful for,
But God's everlasting promise
of life forevermore
Is a reason for thanksgiving
every hour of the day
As we walk toward eternal life
along "the King's highway."

So Many Reasons to Love the Lord

Thank You, God, for little things
    that come unexpectedly
To brighten up a dreary day
    that dawned so dismally.
Thank You, God, for sending
    a happy thought my way
To blot out my depression
    on a disappointing day.
Thank You, God, for brushing
    the dark clouds from my mind
And leaving only sunshine
    and joy of heart behind.
Oh, God, the list is endless
    of things to thank You for,
But I take them all for granted
    and unconsciously ignore
That everything I think or do,
    each movement that I make,
Each measured, rhythmic heartbeat,
    each breath of life I take
Is something You have given me
    for which there is no way
For me in all my smallness
    to in any way repay.

Things to Be Thankful For

The good, green earth
　beneath our feet,
The air we breathe,
　the food we eat,
Some work to do,
　a goal to win,
A hidden longing
　deep within
That spurs us on
　to bigger things
And helps us meet
　what each day brings—
All these things
　and many more
Are things we should
　be thankful for.
And something else
　we should not forget
That people we've known
　or heard of or met
By indirection
　have had a big part
In molding the thoughts
　of the mind and the heart.

And so it's the people
   who are like you
That people like me
   should give thanks to,
For no one can live
   to himself alone
And no one can win
   just on his own.
Too bad there aren't
   a whole lot more
People like you
   to be thankful for.

A Heart Full of Thanksgiving

Everyone needs someone
  to be thankful for,
And each day of life
  we are aware of this more,
For the joy of enjoying
  and the fullness of living
Are found only in hearts
  that are filled with thanksgiving!

Quit Supposin'

Don't start your day by supposin'
    that trouble is just ahead,
It's better to stop supposin'
    and start with a prayer instead,
And make it a prayer of thanksgiving
    for the wonderful things God has wrought
Like the beautiful sunrise and sunset,
    God's gifts that are free and not bought.
For what is the use of supposin'
    the dire things that could happen to you
And worrying about some misfortune
    that seldom if ever comes true?
But instead of just idle supposin'
    step forward to meet each new day
Secure in the knowledge God's near you
    to lead you each step of the way.
For supposin' the worst things will happen
    only helps to make them come true,
And you darken the bright, happy moments
    that the dear Lord has given to you.
So if you desire to be happy
    and get rid of the misery of dread,
Just give up supposin' the worst things
    and look for the best things instead.

May the Lord Bless and Keep You

To be in God's keeping
is surely a blessing,
For though life is often
dark and distressing,
No day is too dark
and no burden too great
That God in His love
cannot penetrate.
And to know and believe
without question or doubt
That no matter what happens
God is there to help out,
Is to hold in your hand
"the golden key"
To peace and to joy
and serenity!

Give Lavishly!
Live Abundantly

The more you give,
  the more you get,
The more you laugh,
  the less you fret,
The more you do
  unselfishly,
The more you live
  abundantly.
The more of everything
  you share,
The more you'll always
  have to spare,
The more you love,
  the more you'll find
That life is good
  and friends are kind.
For only what
  we give away,
Enriches us
  from day to day.

Yesterday, Today, and Tomorrow

Yesterday's dead,
  tomorrow's unborn,
So there's nothing to fear
  and nothing to mourn,
For all that is past
  and all that has been
Can never return
  to be lived once again.
And what lies ahead
  or the things that will be
Are still in God's hands
  so it is not up to me
To live in the future
  that is God's great unknown
For the past and the present
  God claims for His own.

So all I need to do
　　is to live for today
And trust God to show me
　　the truth and the way,
For it's only the memory
　　of things that have been
And expecting tomorrow
　　to bring trouble again
That fills my today,
　　which God wants to bless,
With uncertain fears
　　and borrowed distress.
All I need live for
　　is this one little minute,
For life's here and now
　　and eternity's in it.

A Bend in the Road

When we feel we have nothing to give,
    and we're sure that the song has ended,
When our day seems over and the shadows fall
    and the darkness of night has descended,
Where can we go to find the strength
    to valiantly keep on trying?
Where can we find the hand that will dry
    the tears that the heart is crying?
There's but one place to go and that is to God,
    and dropping all pretense and pride,
We can pour out our problems without restraint
    and gain strength with Him at our side.
And together we stand at life's crossroads
    and view what we think is the end,
But God has a much bigger vision,
    and He tells us it's only a bend,
For the road goes on and is smoother,
    and the pause in the song is a rest,
And the part that's unsung and unfinished
    is the sweetest and richest and best.
So rest and relax and grow stronger,
    let go and let God share your load,
Your work is not finished or ended,
    you've just come to a bend in the road.

Stepping-stones

As birthdays come and go
   and years go swiftly by,
Each one becomes a stepping-stone
   to that promised land on high.
And I look forward happily
   to that life that never ends
Where we can visit endlessly
   with our loved ones and our friends.
So in these troubled days on earth
   I rejoice to know it's true
That someday I'll spend eternity
   With "angels" just like you.

New Beginnings

May your retirement
turn out to be for you
A time of new beginnings
and new dimensions too,
In which you find fulfillment
of your creative art
And joy in every avenue
of spirit, mind, and heart.

Life's Golden Autumn

Birthdays come and birthdays go
   and with them comes the thought
Of all the happy memories
   the passing years have brought.
And looking back across the years
   it's a joy to reminisce,
For memory opens wide the door
   on a happy day like this,
And with a sweet nostalgia
   we longingly recall
The happy days of long ago
   that seem the best of all.
But time cannot be halted
   in its swift and endless flight,
And age is sure to follow youth
   as day comes after night,
And once again it's proven
   that the restless brain of man
Is powerless to alter
   God's great unchanging plan.

But while our step grows slower
    and we grow more tired too,
The soul goes soaring upward
    to realms untouched and new,
For growing older only means
    the spirit grows serene
And we behold things with our souls
    that our eyes have never seen.
So birthdays are but gateways
    to eternal life above
Where God's children live forever
    in the beauty of His love.

The Autumn of Life

What a wonderful time is life's autumn
  when the leaves of the trees are all gold,
When God fills each day as He sends it,
  with memories, priceless and old.
What a treasure house filled with rare jewels
  are the blessings of year upon year,
When life has been lived as you've lived it
  in a home where God's presence is dear.
And may the deep meaning surrounding this day,
  like the paintbrush of God up above,
Touch your life with wonderful blessings
  and fill your heart brimful with love!

WINTER

A Mystery and Miracle

In the beauty of a snowflake
falling softly on the land
Is the mystery and the miracle
of God's great, creative hand.

A Christmas Prayer

God, make us aware
that in Thy name
The holy Christ child
humbly came
To live on earth
and leave behind
New faith and hope
for all mankind.
And make us aware
that the Christmas story
Is everyone's promise
of eternal glory.

Glory to God in the Highest

"Glory to God in the highest
  and peace on earth to men,"
May the Christmas song the angels sang
  stir in our hearts again
And bring a new awareness
  that the fate of every nation
Is sealed securely in the hand
  of the Maker of creation.
For we, with all our knowledge,
  our inventions and our skill,
Can never go an inch beyond
  the holy Father's will.
And all of our achievements
  are so puny and so small,
Just "ant hills" in the kingdom
  of the God who made us all.
For greater than the scope of man
  and far beyond all seeing,
In Him who made the universe,
  we live and have our being.

Behold, I Bring You Good Tidings of Great Joy

Glad tidings herald
   the Christ child's birth—
"Joy to the world"
   and "peace on earth,"
"Glory to God,"
   let all men rejoice
And hearken once more
   to the angel's voice.
It matters not who
   or what you are,
All can behold
   the Christmas star,
For the star that shone
   is shining still
In the hearts of those
   of peace and goodwill.

It offers the answer
    to everyone's need,
Regardless of color
    or race or creed,
So joining together
    in brotherly love,
Let us worship again
    our Father above,
And forgetting our own
    little selfish desires
May we seek what the star
    of Christmas inspires.

The Miracle of Christmas

The wonderment in
   a small child's eyes,
The ageless awe
   in the Christmas skies,
The nameless joy
   that fills the air,
The throngs that kneel
   in praise and prayer . . .
These are the things
   that make us know
That men may come
   and men may go,
But none will
   ever find a way
To banish Christ
   from Christmas Day,
For with each child
   there's born again
A mystery
   that baffles men.

Let Us Keep Christ in Christmas

Christmas is a season
    for joy and merrymaking,
A time for gifts and presents,
    for giving and for taking,
A festive, friendly, happy time
    when everyone is gay,
And cheer, goodwill, and laughter
    are part of Christmas Day.
God wants us to be happy
    on the birthday of His Son,
And that is why this season
    is such a joyous one,
For long ago the angels
    rejoiced at Bethlehem
And so down through the ages
    we have followed after them.
But in our celebrations
    of merriment and mirth
Let's not forget the miracle
    of the holy Christ child's birth,
For in our gay festivities
    It is easy to lose sight
Of the baby in the manger
    and that holy silent night,

For Christmas in this modern world
  is a very different scene
From the stable and the Christ child
  so peaceful and serene.
Now we think of Christmas
  as glittering gifts and such,
Things for eager eyes to see
  and reaching hands to touch,
But we miss the mighty meaning
  and we lose the greater glory
Of the holy little Christ child
  and the blessed Christmas story
If we don't keep Christ in Christmas
  and make His love a part
Of all the joy and happiness
  that fill our home and heart.
Without the holy Christ child
  what is Christmas but a day
That is filled with empty pleasures
  that will only pass away,
But by keeping Christ in Christmas
  we are helping to fulfill
The glad tiding of the angels—
  Peace on earth and goodwill—
and the Father up in heaven
  looking down on earth, will say,
"You have kept Christ in your Christmas,
  now I'll keep you all the way!"

Rejoice! It's Christmas!

May the holy remembrance
    of the first Christmas Day
Be our reassurance
    Christ is not far away.
For on Christmas He came
    to walk here on earth,
So let us find joy
    in the news of His birth.
And let us find comfort
    and strength for each day
In knowing that Christ
    walked this same earthly way.
So He knows all our needs
    and He hears every prayer
And He keeps all His children
    always safe in His care.
And whenever we're troubled
    and lost in despair
We have but to seek Him
    and ask Him in prayer
To guide and direct us
    and help us to bear
Our sickness and sorrow,
    our worry and care.
So once more at Christmas
    let the whole world rejoice
In the knowledge He answers
    every prayer that we voice.

Christmas Is
a Season for Giving

Christmas is a season
    for gifts of every kind,
All the glittering, pretty things
    that Christmas shoppers find.
Baubles, beads, and bangles
    of silver and of gold,
Anything and everything
    that can be bought or sold
Is given at this season
    to place beneath the tree
For Christmas is a special time
    for giving lavishly.
But there's one rare and priceless gift
    that can't be sold or bought,
It's something poor or rich can give
    for it's a loving thought—
And loving thoughts are something
    for which no one can pay,
And only loving hearts can give
    this priceless gift away.

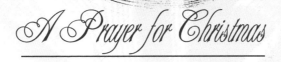

A Prayer for Christmas

God, give us eyes this Christmas
    to see the Christmas star,
And give us ears to hear the song
    of angels from afar,
And with our eyes and ears attuned
    for a message from above,
Let Christmas angels speak to us
    of hope and faith and love—
Hope to light our pathway
    when the way ahead is dark,
Hope to sing through stormy days
    with the sweetness of the lark,
Faith to trust in things unseen
    and know beyond all seeing
That it is in our Father's love
    we live and have our being,
And love to break down barriers
    of color, race, and creed,
Love to see and understand
    and help all those in need.

A New Beginning

It doesn't take a new year
  to begin our lives anew—
God grants us new beginnings
  each day the whole year through.
So never be discouraged
  for there comes daily to all men
The chance to make another start
  and begin all over again!

A New Year!
A New Day!
A New Life!

Not only on New Year's
    but all the year through
God gives us a chance
    to begin life anew,
For each day at dawning
    we have but to pray
That all the mistakes
    we made yesterday
Will be blotted out
    and forgiven by grace,
For God in His love
    will completely efface
All that is past
    and He'll grant a new start
To all who are truly
    repentant at heart.
And well may we pause
    in awesome-like wonder
That our Father in heaven
    who dwells far asunder
Could still remain willing
    to freely forgive

The shabby, small lives
    we so selfishly live
And still would be mindful
    of sin-ridden man
Who constantly goes on
    defying God's plan—
But this is the gift
    of God's limitless love,
A gift that we are
    so unworthy of,
But God gave it to us
    and all we need do
Is to ask God's forgiveness
    and begin life anew.

A Pattern
for the New Year

"Love one another
  as I have loved you"
May seem a task
  impossible to do,
But if you will try
  to trust and believe,
Great are the joys
  that you will receive.
For love makes us patient,
  understanding, and kind,
And we judge with our heart
  and not with our mind.
For as soon as love enters
  the heart's opened door,
The faults we once saw
  are not there anymore,
And the things that seemed wrong
  begin to look right
When viewed in the softness
  of love's gentle light.

Love works in ways
   that are wondrous and strange,
for there is nothing in life
   that love cannot change,
And all that God promised
   will someday come true
When you love one another
   the way He loved you.

Deep in My Heart

Happy little memories
　　go flitting through my mind,
And in all my thoughts and memories
　　I always seem to find
The picture of your face, dear,
　　the memory of your touch
And all the other little things
　　I've come to love so much.
You cannot go beyond my thoughts
　　or leave my love behind
Because I keep you in my heart
　　and forever on my mind,
And though I may not tell you,
　　I think you know it's true,
That I find daily happiness
　　in the very thought of you.

Show Me the Way

God, help me in my own small way
To somehow do something each day
To show You that I love You best
And that my faith will stand each test.
And let me serve You every day
And feel You near me when I pray.
Oh, hear my prayer, dear God above,
And make me worthy of Your love.